Hong Kong – Last Prize of the Empire
1991 Hong Kong Book of the Year Award

© FormAsia Books Limited
Published by FormAsia Books Limited
2301 Sunning Plaza, 10 Hysan Avenue
Hong Kong

1st Edition 1991
2nd Edition 1993

Written by Trea Wiltshire
Proofread by Geraldine Christie
Designed by Ian Leung/Format Limited
Printed in Hong Kong
by Hong Kong Prime Printing Co Ltd

Photographic acknowledgements:
The Peabody Museum Massachusetts, Margaret Lee – The HongkongBank, Arthur Hacker – The Stockhouse Ltd., Public Records Library Hong Kong, Benno Gross Associates, Government Information Services Hong Kong, Filan and Andrew Denman, Sister Pauline – St Paul de Chartre, The Peak Tramways Co. Ltd., Judy Young – The South China Morning Post Ltd., D. P. Franklin, Jay Green – St John's Cathedral Bookstore, P.G. Popham, Chris Keeping, Veronica and Ron Clibborn-Dyer, T.A. Horstler – The Star Ferry Co. Ltd., Teresa Coleman Fine Arts, Amanda Lack – Altfield Gallery, Peter Moss, Maisie Shun-Wah – Cathay Pacific Airways Ltd., Honeychurch Antiques Hong Kong, Sian Griffiths and Christina Cheng – The Peninsula Hotel, Sid Hookham, Grace Lui – Constitutional Affairs Branch, Jean Butler – The Foreign and Commonwealth Office, Tony Boase, The Public Records Library Kew.

HONG KONG
LAST PRIZE OF THE EMPIRE

by Trea Wiltshire

FormAsia

HONG KONG – LAST PRIZE OF THE EMPIRE

by Trea Wiltshire

*I*n the 1840s, a decade coloured by exploration, conquest and trade – and the hope and glory of Empire – four Catholic Sisters of the Order of St Paul de Chartres left the mellow security of their convent walls to sail half way across the world.

Their destination was a fever-infested island in the South China Sea that was destined to become one of the glittering prizes of Empire.

Wrested from a reluctant China in the notorious Opium Wars that launched the decade, Hong Kong's cession to Victoria Alexandrina, Queen Empress, symbolized the eclipse of the once-mighty Middle Kingdom by a remote island empire forging its own imperial glory.

When the Sisters embarked from England, their images of China would have been steeped in the mystique that enveloped the vast and ancient Middle Kingdom.

On the dockside they may have caught snatches of the spirited sea shanties that celebrated the beauty and speed of the tea clippers that rode the monsoons to bring the new season's leaf from Cathay to Mincing Lane.

During the four-month voyage to the island moored off the southern sweep of the China coast, they may have heard whispers of the legendary lifestyles of Hong Kong's merchant princes who amassed fortunes from China's fragrant teas, shimmering silks – and the sap of crimson poppies that bloomed in British Bengal and was dried and smuggled into China to feed the opium dreams of its addicts.

They would certainly have seen caricatures of the curious Dragon Emperor who surrounded himself with eunuchs and the high walls of the Forbidden City, issuing edicts with a vermilion brush.

The Emperor exhorted foreign merchants to "Tremble and Obey!" – for China treated all foreign nations as vassal states to the Middle Kingdom. He rejected their persistent attempts to sell China what he contemptuously described as "the manufactures of outside barbarians". He further implored their Queen Empress to strengthen her loyalty and swear perpetual obedience to his Celestial Empire.

Victoria Alexandrina, responding instead to disgruntled diplomats and frustrated merchants, decided to dispatch her imperial forces to defend her nation's "ancient rights of commerce".

In dispute was a quantity of opium chests confiscated from the British merchants by one of the few Chinese officials not profiting from the elaborate system of "squeeze" that allowed "foreign mud" to be traded up and down the China coast. Indeed the Sisters, to their chagrin, might well have heard tales of an over-zealous missionary who acted as interpreter on vessels that dispensed both opium and bibles.

When the nuns were still secure in their convent, scarlet-uniformed troops were sent to overpower ill-equipped Chinese forts, while the British Navy was scuttling ramshackle imperial naval junks that sank with cannons firing and gongs clanging.

The fact that Britain's "ancient rights of commerce" included, in this instance, smuggled opium did not dampen the zeal of the triumphant troops, nor dilute the pomp and ceremony that surrounded the raising of the British Standard on an alien tropical island, far from home in 1841 – a year before the Treaty of Nanking was signed.

When the Sisters approached their destination seven years later, they must have been sustained by the potent promise of the island that seemed to float between the azure of sea and sky.

Mist wreathed the green dragon hills of China and clung to the stern granite crest that dominated the island. Birds called from the depths of hidden valleys, and blue bays with crescents of sand welcomed the travel-worn voyagers.

As their sailing ship entered harbour, it must have been apparent that, for the merchants, the island's promise was already being realized. Trading ships from across the world – some 700 would enter the harbour that year – lay on a swathe of blue almost entirely girdled by tropical greenery.

Rake-masted opium clippers, the pride of the merchant princes, lay at anchor near the private jetties of the major trading hongs. East Indiamen – merchant vessels armed with guns that could give a good account of themselves in any skirmish with imperial Chinese naval junks or local pirates – were surrounded by clusters of craft offering a range of floating services from laundry to barbershops. Hybrid lorchas – with European hulls and Chinese sails; butterfly-sailed fishing junks; barges loaded with stores; and busy, bucking sampans – all added colour and clamour to the harbour scene.

On the waterfront itself, graceful colonnaded

colonial buildings lined the praya and churches, a neoclassical post office, clubs, a courthouse and parade ground could be glimpsed. However, on the outskirts of this tropical replica of Victorian England there were colourful street markets, close-packed shanties, dingy buildings, narrow streets full of mingled aromas, and porcelain-tiled temples wreathed with the smoke of incense. Polite society cocooned itself from this jostling, noisy section of the city by travelling in swift-moving sedan chairs; retreating to colonial clubs with punkahs and fine port; and partaking of cold joints and game pies in the cool interiors of wood-panelled colonial mansions.

Hong Kong blended the Victorian gentility of its colonial administrators with the freebooting, free trade philosophies of its most aggressive foreign traders. They were soon joined by shrewd Chinese merchants, quick to exploit the security of a trading base free from the civil strife, famine and floods of their homeland. Some would make fortunes and achieve considerable status from acting as compradors or intermediaries for foreign merchants trading with China.

Opium smugglers were quick to exploit the hypocrisy of colonial officials who frowned on opium smuggling, yet allowed it to flourish – and indeed to provide the finance for some of its proudest civic achievements. The shrewd Scots, Jardine and Matheson, had encountered the same hypocrisy when smuggling opium into Canton beneath the greedy gaze of corrupt officials who made a charade out of enforcing the Emperor's edicts. So when the colonial government asserted it would offer no protection to smugglers who dealt in the disreputable drug, Matheson wrote contemptuously: "I believe it is like the Chinese edicts, meaning nothing and only meant for the saints in England".

Matheson's mansion on an East Point site, purchased at the colony's first land auction in 1841, commanded the finest view of the harbour from a tree-shaded hillside. With its parterre garden, its chef from St James Street, its cellars full of fine wines and stables of racehorses, it could have been plucked from an estate in Scotland.

But it was not to a mansion such as this that the four Sisters repaired on arrival. Their few belongings would have been carried on shoulder poles by lean, sinewy coolies, while they retreated modestly behind the curtains of sedan chairs.

The Sisters arrival would have stirred much curiosity for their habit was distinctive and the starched white coifs that framed their calm faces reminded onlookers of lotus flowers. When the Sisters headed, not for punkah-cooled comfort, but for a humid hillside shack in Wan Chai, locals appreciated that they were dealing with women of rare spirit.

Initially the Sisters, conforming to Chinese custom, ventured out as little as Chinese women who seldom saw the world that lay beyond their high-walled homes. However, word soon spread that they were the friends of the poor and destitute. They sent a local priest out into the streets each day to collect abandoned children – babies in ragged bundles; unwanted girls; small, emaciated bodies racked with fever and thought to be possessed by vengeful spirits. Some survived barely long enough to be baptised in the orphanage.

However, the Sisters quickly appreciated that they needed the support of the community in which they operated, and soon their distinctive coifs and calm faces were a familiar sight against the backdrop of the city's slums. When English ladies learnt of their work, they hastened to place orders for needlework – for the orphans were instructed in embroidery and fancy work to enable them to earn a living.

Before the end of the decade, the mission of the Order of St Paul de Chartres was well established and the Sisters were fulfilling the promise that had originally lured them from well-ordered peace to a tenuous existence where they dealt with death on a daily basis.

Though fever would claim the life of one within a few years, the trio that remained were undeterred, evincing a will to survive that was shaped not only by their faith, but by the island itself.

Hong Kong's philosophy for survival was honed by the trauma that marked its fledgling years.

Angry typhoons lashed the island, fire frequently consumed its townsite and fever ravaged its population. But it had lured a breed of men and women who gambled against the odds of ending up beneath a headstone in the colonial cemetery or in a coffin destined for burial in China.

Of necessity, the island adopted a brazen effrontery that belied its size and the vulnerability of its situation in the shadow of a giant host that initially plotted its demise on a daily basis.

When the Emperor was told of the untimely typhoon that totally destroyed its first townsite – all but Matheson's opium warehouse – he immediately repaired to the temple to give thanks to Heaven, only to be informed that the city of Victoria was being reconstructed with renewed vigour.

Like the Sisters of St Paul de Chartres, those who came to the colony – merchants, missionaries or colonial officials – were sustained by its promise.

Foreign traders assessed the island's superb harbour and location in terms of mercantile might and personal wealth. Missionaries saw it as a base from which they could nurture faiths that would sometimes fuel resentment in China. Queen Victoria's colonial officials calculated that a British presence on the very edge of the Middle Kingdom would serve as a reminder of its naval and military superiority – and of its determination to open up China to a fast-changing world of technology and trade that was unfolding beyond its borders.

While Hong Kong clearly held the promise of hope and glory for Britain, its cession was not without advantage to China. Though its loss was a source of humiliation, it had to be admitted that the island which even the British Foreign Secretary had dubbed "a barren rock" had been all but ignored by the mandarin in whose province it lay.

By conceding to Britain's demands for a trading base, China kept at least some of the barbarian traders off shore. Peking had always displayed a high contempt for those who pursued profit so zealously. "They look upon trade as their chief occupation", noted one disapproving court official, "and are wanting in any high purpose".

China also clearly profited from the barbarian demand for teas and silks, for silver bullion from Britain helped to satisfy a taste for fine porcelain and silks among corrupt officials, and to sustain the extravagance of those who dwelt in the Forbidden City and had no concept of the stark realities of life beyond its fairy-tale lakes, pavilions and high, porcelain-tiled walls.

From its earliest years Hong Kong learnt to live by the precepts that defined its tenuous existence. It quickly nurtured an unflinching will to survive – and appreciated that survival lay in exploiting the best and worst of its two imperial masters.

Initially location was its lure, but it would both profit – and be plagued by – its situation on the doorstep of China. Umbilically linked with the mainland, it would suffer the aftermath of every drought, famine or rebellion that racked its neighbour.

The high-minded fanaticism and wholesale slaughter of the Taiping Rebellion of the 1850s brought the first wave of hungry and homeless. The collapse of the 268-year-old Manchu dynasty, the last to rule China, ignited attacks on foreigners, an assassination attempt on a new colonial governor, and the arrival of reinforcements from British India.

The civil turmoil that followed China's declaration of the Republic in 1911 – its division by warlords, rapacious foreign interests and opposing political factions, and its descent into financial chaos – brought boycotts, strikes, more refugees, and mounting unease.

When in 1949, amid a sea of red silk flags, Mao Zedong promised: "Our country will never again be an insulted nation. The Chinese people have stood up ...", a steady surge of people headed south to the British Crown Colony of Hong Kong. Just as foreign merchants had once used the island as a safe base from which to make trading forays into China, so now the Chinese people used it as a temporary refuge; a stepping stone to the outside world; a new home free from the revolutionary dogma and the rigid ideology that gripped their homeland.

In Hong Kong, when the flag of the People's Republic was run up five yards from the British border amid a barrage of firecrackers, the colony took on the tattered, desperate appearance of a human life raft. Dingy tenements were crammed with refugees, hillsides were littered with makeshift homes, and health services were stretched to the limit as the colony counted as many as 10,000 new arrivals in a single week.

Later, the devastating economic effects of the Great Leap Forward brought another wave of refugees that threatened to engulf the colony until, of necessity, barbed-wire barricades were erected to stem the hungry human flood.

A further exercise in revolution followed,

climaxing in a reign of terror that would prompt daring escapes across the border and erupt into riots on the streets of Hong Kong.

During the Cultural Revolution, water restrictions added to the tensions that charged the city during the long, hot summer of 1967. Riots choked its streets with tear gas; unsmiling protesters chanted Communist slogans beneath the unflinching gaze of British guards at Government House; bombs left pools of blood and torn limbs in streets which could swiftly turn into battlegrounds.

The summer of '67 deep-etched Hong Kong's anomalous plight in the minds of its residents – and a fascinated world that watched the tiny unashamedly capitalist colony heading for a confrontation with its communist landlord.

Hong Kong's vulnerability had never seemed so acute.

It was a gaudy patch sewn to the homespun fabric of China; a colony that persisted long after the twilight of Empire; a thriving industrial city with no resources but the untiring energy of its people; a financial centre dependant on confidence and stability – but one that carried a timepiece set to self-destruct in a matter of decades; a territory supporting over five million people whose ideology was diametrically opposed to that of a landlord on whom it was dependant for food, water, its very existence. It was a city sustained by rags to riches dreams, yet one that never for a minute lost sight of the stark realities of survival.

As the stock market plummeted, nervous millionaires packed their bags for a sojourn somewhere safer, and an unusually large number of government officials and Legislative Councillors took leave or found it necessary to travel overseas. Those who had nowhere to go watched the confrontation and waited for it to be resolved – and were occasionally entertained by the battle of nerves.

At the height of the riots, while white-flannelled colonials attempted to shed their angst on the emerald patch of the Hong Kong Cricket Club that stretched beneath the communist Bank of China, they were subjected to a stream of cacophonous propaganda. Such an occasion summoned the best in the British – not only did the game proceed, with the players hardly deigning to glance at the bank festooned with red banners, but the neighbouring British bank decided to disturb the peace further by broadcasting the National Anthem and other spirited refrains.

The summer of discontent ended with the season – and China's honouring of an agreement, signed a few years earlier, to supply Hong Kong with 15,000 million gallons of water between October and June each year. Hong Kong wags had long observed that if China ever wanted to reclaim Hong Kong all it would have to do was make a phone call. However, the call that came on 1st October – the anniversary of the People's Republic of China – politely enquired whether the colony was ready to receive water from the East River.

Even while capitalist and communist were confronting one another in the summer of '67, those with a steady hand and an eye for the main chance, including investors from the mainland, were buying up under-valued real estate and the businesses of those whose nerve had failed as the tear gas hung in the air and the mood of the city darkened.

Hong Kong had been nurtured by adversity. "The people have learnt to live with bad news", was the wry observation of a seasoned investor studying the nervous stock market after the June 1989 protests in Tiananmen Square.

The Cantonese word for crisis – 危機 – combines elements of both danger and opportunity, and from the outset the colony's most visionary businessmen showed that they could turn disaster to profit. When the Korean War threatened its economic lifeline as an entrepôt, refugees engulfed the tiny territory, and British socialists suggested it should be handed back to China as part of a trade agreement. Hong Kong, its back to the wall, fought back the only way it knew how.

With Cantonese money, Shanghainese industrial know-how, the *laissez faire* policies of the colonial government, Hong Kong put to work its hungry and homeless. The world watched an instant industrial revolution in the making, and marvelled at an "economic miracle" that Hong Kong appreciated was fuelled by enterprise and energy, sweat and sacrifice.

Hong Kong has always relished its capacity to surprise the world – with its ability to survive, its track record of doing things faster or better than its rivals, or with the sheer scale and audacity of its latest projects.

It enjoys what appears to be the rash bravado of planning an ambitious new airport facility, with attendant tunnels, highways, rail links and a suspension bridge, and extensive reclamation projects that run well into the next century while the spectre of 1997 advances daily. Yet hard-nosed instincts underlie what sometimes seems like the old, bold effrontery of a colonial island born of Empire.

In 1984, British Prime Minister Margaret Thatcher, with the Governor of Hong Kong at her side, signed the fourth and last Anglo-Chinese treaty on Hong Kong. The Joint Declaration established that on 1st July 1997 Hong Kong would become a Special Administrative Region of the People's Republic of China. Though China will reassert its sovereignty over Hong Kong, it has agreed to respect the colony's laws and lifestyle, plus the capitalist traditions that have for so long driven its buoyant economy.

Survival now depends on convincing China that it is inheriting a quite extraordinary economic asset, but one that will become a gleaming, empty shell if confidence and capital take flight. It depends on persuading China's leadership that the infusion of colour and capitalist ways that Hong Kong and other foreign investment is already generating in neighbouring Guangzhou province, will not undermine its authority. It depends on the conviction that a communist country that has already succumbed to Coca-Cola and credit cards, won't regress to hard-line revolutionary dogma. It depends on both China and Hong Kong learning to live with one another –

a process that began back in 1842 when China agreed, in the Treaty of Nanking, not to refer to the British as "barbarians" in official documents, and when, in 1896, the colony first charted its apolitical course by expelling a young revolutionary – Sun Yat-sen – for stirring dissent against China's crumbling Manchu dynasty.

Ambitious, grand-scale infrastructure projects such as the new airport – which will rank as the world's most expensive construction project ever conceived – and plans to upgrade port facilities, clearly buttress Hong Kong's status as the commercial gateway to southern China. Already the colony has replaced Rotterdam as the world's busiest container port. Already it rivals Manhattan, London and Tokyo as a global financial centre.

Although technically still a British colony, Hong Kong has largely shed its colonial mantle to become a global city, an international entity in itself. Its dollar is pegged to the US currency, its biggest investors are the United States, China and Japan, and its tastes are truly international.

Today the waterfront, that a century ago was enhanced by graceful colonial buildings, is dramatized by shimmering towers of commerce comprising American glass, German steel, Japanese air conditioners, Swiss elevators and Sicilian marble – with perhaps a Henry Moore in the foyer.

Today, the city consumes more French cognac and boasts more Rolls-Royces per head of population than any other city. Stroll through Queen's Road Central's smart arcades and you'll encounter Gucci,

Hermès, Louis Vuitton, Nina Ricci, Charles Jourdan, Van Cleef and Arpels. Stroll further down to the alleys and you'll find clever counterfeits for those who can't afford the originals.

The colony's commercial heart presents a stunning spectacle of corporate high-rise created by some of the world's most celebrated contemporary architects. Within the sweep of a single glance, your eye is arrested by the slender aluminium and glass sheath of the Bank of China by Chinese-American architect I. M. Pei; British architect Sir Norman Foster's futuristic fantasy of tubes and girders for the HongkongBank; the hexagonal, multifaceted glass "sculptures" of the Lippo Centre by America's Paul Rudolph.

Hong Kong's cityscape has become an amazing collection of steel and glass towers – blue, silver, white and cobalt – that reflect one another and the changing hues of the sky, and are as exciting to camera-totting travellers as its other major attractions.

Dwarfed by the towers are a few reminders of an earlier era that have somehow survived in a city without sentiment for the past. In Central, there is the imposing dome of the old Supreme Court that now accommodates the Legislative Council. Across the harbour, the Peninsula Hotel continues to lure patrons with handsome silver tea services, glinting glasses and a late afternoon string quartet that fills the cream and gold lobby with the nostalgia of an era of grace and elegance. In Causeway Bay, there is another dome that has stood for many decades –

that of St Paul's Cathedral. Its survival as the centrepiece of a hospital and school complex is testimony to the commitment of those who continue to fulfil the promise of an Order established by four Sisters in the first decade of Hong Kong's life.

The orphans are long gone, but children's voices still rise around the granite dome of St Paul's as they always have. And the Sisters, with their calm faces and starched white habits, still count their rosaries beneath the shade of old banyans in the precinct gardens.

While the Sisters of St Paul have always faced an uncertain future comforted by their faith, Hong Kong has always pushed the thought of 1997 to the back of its collective psyche. Now, however, 1997 is the currency of conversation, generating debate among both pessimists and optimists.

Pessimists revive the horror of Tiananmen Square in 1989 and point to the fact that the People's Liberation Army will be garrisoned in Hong Kong.

Optimists claim that China will honour its commitment to "One Country Two Systems" and non-interference in Hong Kong's affairs for half a century. In their minds 1997 has been replaced, as the crucial date, by 2047.

Pessimists allude to the possibility of radical zealots lurking in the wings of China's political stage; optimists view 1997 as an eternity away, in political terms – time enough for the emergence of a Sino version of Gorbachev.

Pessimists point to the haemorrhage of young talent as immigration queues form outside foreign embassies; optimists cite the number who return – contingency passports secure in their briefcases – to chase the fortunes that can still be made in Hong Kong.

Pessimists cite the unpredictability of China as Hong Kong's greatest threat; optimists take the line that with the two economies interlocking in so many areas, China is unlikely to jeopardise the economic success of its biggest customer and investor.

Both would acknowledge that Hong Kong has, over the years, provided China with an arena in which it could try its hand at capitalism. And mainland communists have proved themselves adept at making profits. Today, China's financial stake in Hong Kong runs into billions of dollars and 35 per cent of its foreign currency passes through the Bank of China in Hong Kong.

But while some debate, analyse and plan strategy, others take a more fatalistic approach, for although Hong Kong's façade may be impressively international, at least part of its soul remains steadfastly traditional. It will burn joss sticks at the shrines of innumerable gods to buy its survival.

It will consult countless fortune-tellers, listening again to the legend of the 12 zodiac animals that shape both the years they rule and the lives of those born under their signs.

It is said that when the Lord Buddha was preparing to leave Earth, he summoned all the animals to bid him farewell. Only 12 came and he named a year after each in the order of their arrival. The opportunist Rat was first.

The Rat, a self-proclaimed acquisitor, strikes its target with swift, unerring intent. "Each search must end in a new quest", runs the poem that describes him.

The year of the Rat is said to be a year of plenty, a year for opportunists.

Though marked by fluctuation and speculation, fortunes can be made, and wealth accumulated.

In the Chinese lunar calendar, the longest chronological record in history, the Year of the Rat, the acquisitor, fell in 1984 – the year in which the Joint Declaration sealed the fate of Britain's last major colony, its last prize of Empire.

All that remains to be revealed is the identity of the acquisitor when at midnight on 30th June 1997, the British flag is lowered for the last time, the border dissolves – and China is exposed to the world's most celebrated bastion of unbridled capitalism.

"A Little England in the Eastern Seas …"

The heyday of Empire saw the production and dispatch – to far-flung colonial outposts – of an impressive array of imperial statuary.

The Queen Empress, in sombre widow's weeds, and the princes and princesses of a remote island kingdom, gazed down on their subject races from domed canopies shading them from the merciless noonday sun.

Raggio's bronze of Victoria Alexandrina, destined for Royal Square, seemed to reflect the Queen's initial displeasure at her acquisition, as one of the spoils of the Opium Wars, of a barren island that her Foreign Secretary assured her would never become a mart of trade. However, by the time her bronze replica was unveiled to mark her jubilee in 1887, the Empress had no doubt amended her early dismissal of Hong Kong as something of a royal joke: "Albert is so much amused at my having got the island of Hong Kong…", she had quipped in 1841. When her grandsons later visited the fast-growing colony they assured her that the barren rock had been miraculously transformed into "a little England in the Eastern Seas, a creation of British energy, enterprise and industry".

In fact, Raggio's bronze evinced as much will to survive as the colony itself. During the Japanese occupation the Great White Queen, Sir Thomas Jackson, an early chairman of the Hongkong and Shanghai Bank, and other colonial statuary were unceremoniously dispatched to Japan to be melted down for armaments. However, the stern-faced Queen and the moustachiod banker, both so symbolic of the colony, survived. The banker was restored to Statue Square (*following pages*), while the former Queen (*above*), surveys the last major outpost of her once-powerful empire from a leafy corner of Victoria Park – remote from the political and commercial heart of Hong Kong. 🦁

Of Politics and Blind Justice

*I*n 1903, work began on the imposing domed Supreme Court, designed by Aston Webb, which was built on the reclaimed land of the Praya Central. Today the court building, mounted by the statue of Blind Justice, is the political centre of Hong Kong, accommodating the Legislative Council which, along with the Executive Council, serves as a quasi-parliament.

The Supreme Court building is one of the few landmarks in the heart of the city to have survived decades of dramatic change. Another is the bronze statue of Sir Thomas Jackson, who guided the destiny of the Hongkong and Shanghai Bank from 1866 to 1902. Whereas statues of British royalty have been removed from Statue Square, "Lucky" Jackson, so much a symbol of the commercial impulse that took root in Hong Kong, still surveys the former court, its contemporary neighbours and the busy harbour beyond.

From Colonial to Contemporary

*F*uturistic architecture and dazzling glass towers reflect the ever-changing face of Queen's Road Central, one of the world's most expensive stretches of real estate. This major thoroughfare through the commercial heart of Hong Kong is lined with a luxury hotel, major banks, office blocks and shops. Well-heeled locals and tourists cast acquisitive eyes on luxury items displayed in the immaculately dressed windows of Van Cleef and Arpels, Chanel, Gucci, Nina Ricci and other exclusive international stores.

Further west, however, the busy road sheds its chic and becomes more characteristically Hong Kong, with jostling, bargaining crowds moving through smaller shops and down narrow alleys packed with stalls. Queen's Road has more than fulfilled the dreams of Victorian entrepreneurs who knew it as a narrow track along the waterfront.

Later it was flanked by graceful colonial architecture and an imposing clock tower – donated by one of its eminent citizens – which aroused considerable controversy and was finally declared a traffic hazard, and removed.

Given the pace of change, this famous road may well have acquired a new face by the 21st century – even, perhaps, a new name. 🦁

Wheels of Fortune

Prior to the arrival of the colony's first cars, around 1910, the size, embellishments and livery of one's sedan chair and its bearers served to illustrate one's status. However, the appearance of motor vehicles on the colony's modest stretches of paved roads hastened the eclipse of both the sedan and the rickshaw, and spurred the Government to construct a road that girdled the island.

As early as 1910 an ill-fated forerunner of today's bus service was introduced by the Victoria Motor Car Company. Passengers, up to seven at a time, were offered transport in "a hill-climbing motor car" which, perhaps, was ultimately defeated by a combination of steep gradients and tropical heat.

However, by the 1920s both buses and taxis were available, and if you wished to take a private car across the harbour, a lighter, ordered a day in advance, would come alongside the waterfront to ferry the car over and back.

Later in the decade, lorries would threaten the livelihood of the coolies who had hitherto transported everything – baskets laden with fresh flowers or highly polished grand pianos – from the bamboo poles that rested on their shoulders.

For Hong Kong, cars became – and have remained – status symbols to be flaunted on congested streets and outside exclusive hotels, clubs and stores. Today, the city relishes the notion that it leads the world in per capita ownership of a car that epitomizes unashamed wealth and unquestionable pedigree: Britain's Rolls-Royce. 🏵

The Manpower Carriage

The rickshaw first passed into the imagery of Hong Kong in the 1870s – a Japanese import that would enjoy decades of popularity before it was eased off the streets by an expanded public transport system, the congestion of Hong Kong's traffic – and the discomfort that patrons increasingly felt while being pulled through the streets by old men with tired hearts. In the early years of the 20th century, however, the *jinriksha*, or "manpowered carriage", and the sedan chair were part of the domestic establishment of most of the colony's wealthy families. In 1917, there were over two thousand rickshaws on the island and Kowloon.

Most were public hire, but companies and individuals – and even brothels – often boasted their own private carriages. The last public sedan chair licence expired in 1962 and the last private rickshaw licence seven years later. The latter was held by a company that maintained its vehicle merely to retain the services of its ageing puller. In the 1990s, only a handful of the familiar red carriages survive – as props for tourists keen to have a picture of a mode of transport that has become a curiosity from another era. The rickshaw will undoubtedly pass from the every day street scenes of Hong Kong as will the old men who currently sit idly between their shaffs – for no new licences are being issued. 🦁

The Spirit of the Dragon

*I*n British Hong Kong the dragon, China's most potent symbol, became part of the spectacle of Empire. His spirit was evoked in the serpentine ferocity of Dragon Dances that snaked through the streets in the wake of plumed helmets and parades. On the occasion of King George V's coronation in 1911, an immense dragon with snapping jaws and bulging eyes – activated by 100 sweating dancers – gyrated down Queen's Road Central. The presence of the dragon, emblem of eastern emperors, promised an auspicious inauguration to the reign of England's new king. 🦁

25

Of Cricket and T'ai Chi

*I*n old Hong Kong the racecourse, parade ground, polo and cricket grounds all lay to the east of the city. Later, the imposing granite of the Hongkong and Shanghai Bank overlooked the green expanse of the Hong Kong Cricket Club where the sound of willow striking leather and sporadic applause punctuated long golden afternoons. When the Bank of China – symbol of China's presence in Hong Kong – was erected it had a grandstand view of the urbane white-flannelled cricketers. In 1967, when China's Cultural Revolution spawned riots in Hong Kong through a long, hot summer, mainland propaganda boomed across the cricket grounds from the slogan-plastered bank building. But the cricketers pursued their time-honoured passion and were only mildly distracted when, in response, the neighbouring Hongkong and Shanghai Bank took to broadcasting loud and spirited renditions of the National Anthem.

Today the cricketers are long gone, dispatched to a less visible corner of the island, and their swathe of green has truly become a people's park – Chater Gardens. In the pale light of dawn, as military and naval personnel

raise the flags at the nearby Cenotaph, the day begins in the gardens with the slow measured movements of t'ai chi performed, with many variations, by the elderly. Some go through their graceful ritual in groups, following a leader whose skills set him apart. Others, standing on sheets of the morning newspaper, seek out solitary green alcoves where the chatter of noisy cicadas masks the sound of mounting traffic and busy sparrows hunt for breakfast in small patches of lawn. And the old men and women are as oblivious to the gathering momentum of the city around them as the smart young men and women who cut through this pocket of green, briefcases and designer bags in hand, their minds already on the business of the day ahead. 🦁

Symbol of Collective Sorrow

Since it was unveiled, with colonial pomp, on 11th November 1923, by Governor Sir Mathew Nathan, the Cenotaph has been the scene of some of the city's most impressive, and moving, ceremonies. Annually it is the centre of Remembrance Day services and the laying of wreaths honouring the fallen soldiers of two world wars. But in June of 1989 the Cenotaph became in a single day – and for the first time – the symbol of a collective sorrow that united all the people of Hong Kong and drew them to the city's most familiar monument of mourning (*following pages*).

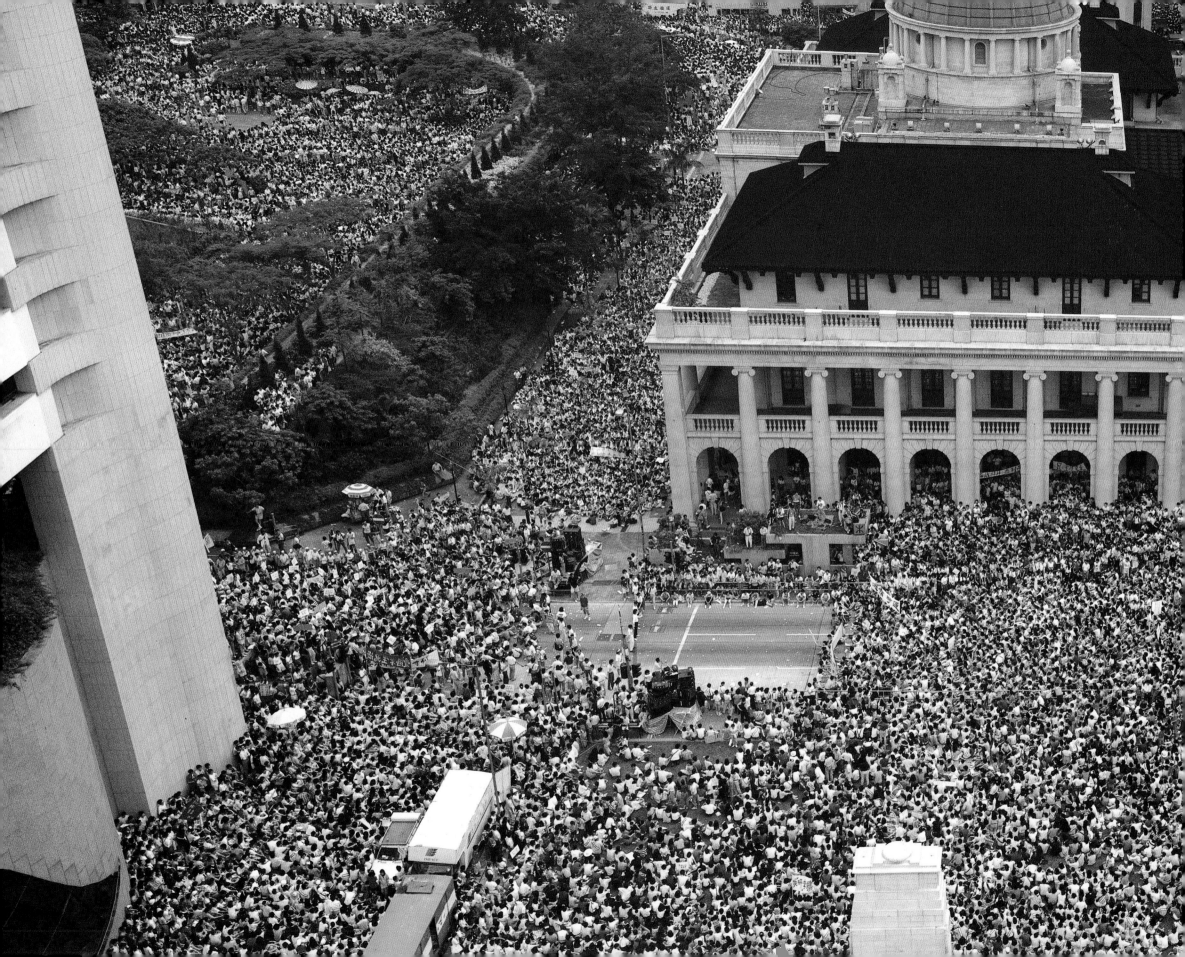

On that day there were no flags. Just tears. Words of bitter disbelief and others of hope scrawled on hastily made posters. And the black-and-white arm and headbands that suddenly appeared on all who converged on the crowded square throughout a stifling summer day and a candlelit night.

But there were wreaths to honour the young Chinese students who had died on Bloody Sunday, along with their dream of democracy, when tanks and troops stormed Tiananmen Square. "We were fighting for the same thing", said one local university student. "If China has no democracy, then Hong Kong has no democracy". So when thousands gathered at the Cenotaph they were mourning not only China's loss but their own.

Days later wreaths and flowers and posters still scattered the Cenotaph steps and the image of them will linger as a reminder of a day – June 4 – which will loom almost as large as 1997 in the minds of Hong Kong people. For it acknowledged the ideals that linked mainland communist with colonial capitalist – ideals which in themselves made even concepts like One Country Two Systems seem of secondary importance. ❧

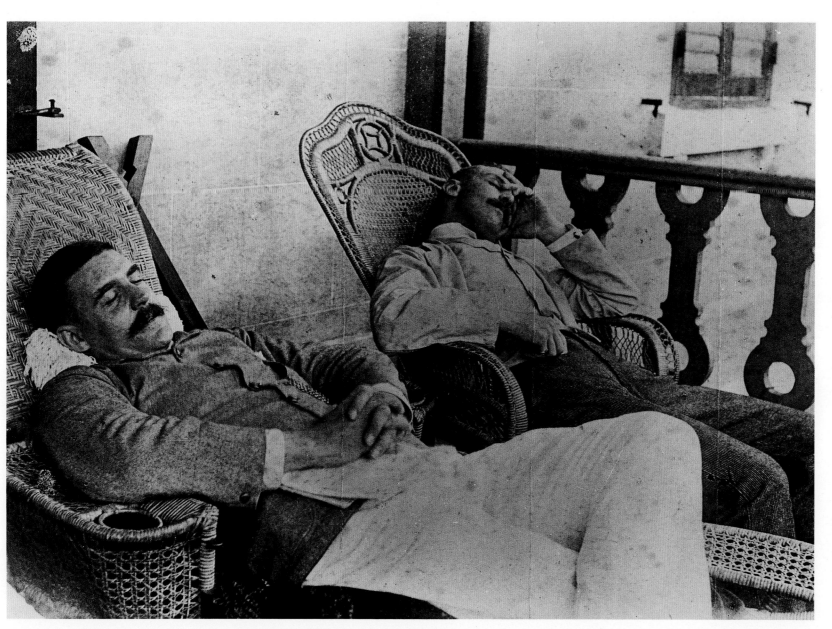

A Colonial Retreat

At the height of Empire, colonial clubs were the pivot of social life in eastern outposts. The tea planter in Ceylon, the taipan in Hong Kong or the colonial official overwhelmed by the task of administering history's largest empire – all could retreat to the Club where leather and chinz, wood-panelled libraries and a cellar of fine port allowed them to nurture dreams of the mellow comforts of "home" while briefly abandoning the White Man's Burden.

Colonial clubs were often unashamedly exclusive, reinforcing the clearly defined social strata and rigid codes scrupulously observed in Victorian England. Much to their chagrin or outrage, many who applied to join the Club were flatly refused membership.

The Hong Kong Club, the oldest in the colony, was formed in 1844, and was initially situated on Wyndham Street.

A handsome new three-storey Club, all chandeliers, fluted columns and "the right sort of people" was built in 1897. It was finally demolished in 1981 and the Club is now accommodated over several well-appointed floors in a building as contemporary as its predecessor was classic. 🦁

Flower Street

Imported trees and luxuriant shrubbery soon transformed the "barren rock" while flower gardens added bright patches to the Kowloon peninsula. Flower sellers gathered in Wyndham Street in the city's commercial heart and as the price of blooms fell, the bright baskets spread further and further up the street, shaded by spreading banyan trees. Members of the nearby Hong Kong Club could always be cajoled to buy a button hole from the flower sellers who converged on its entrance. Vivid colours and beguiling perfumes from flower stalls still linger in Wyndham Street, though few would remember that it was once called Flower Street.

Traders in Tea and Silk

*H*ong Kong has always lived by trade. Taipans traded in tea, silk and opium with Chinese compradors acting as their intermediaries. From its earliest days it was obvious that Hong Kong was destined to become an eastern entrepôt of untold potential, its harbour was filled with majestic clipper ships loading and off-loading the merchandise of China and Britain, and its townsite was soon crowded with small open-fronted stores selling fragrant Chinese teas, incense for the temples and other merchandise valued by the growing Chinese community. The growth of the China trade greatly enhanced the social status of Chinese merchants once considered on a humble par with actors in the hierarchy of Chinese society. A handful of traditional Chinese shops, often handed down through generations, still survive in Hong Kong – like this incense shop – but their future is tenuous in a city which today fills its shop windows with the fads, fashions and technology of the 20th century.

Messages from the Gods

*I*solated above the fledgling townsite of Victoria, the Man Mo Temple once lured worshippers up a narrow track that mounted the lower flanks of the Peak. Later, stone ladder streets climbed the sheer hillside to the incense-wreathed temple with its distinctive tiled rooftop crowned with an elaborate pantheon of porcelain figurines. Built in the first few years of the colony's life, the temple's backdrop was a tapestry of tropical greenery.

Later, the city began to crowd around it, and finally to dwarf it. Yet in the dim tranquillity of its smoke-blackened interior the embrace of the contemporary city recedes. Fortune-tellers interpret messages from the gods, offerings are placed on the alters of the two Taoist gods to whom the temple is dedicated, and sweet-scented incense hangs above century-old brass burners and drifts from the huge coils suspended from the rafters.

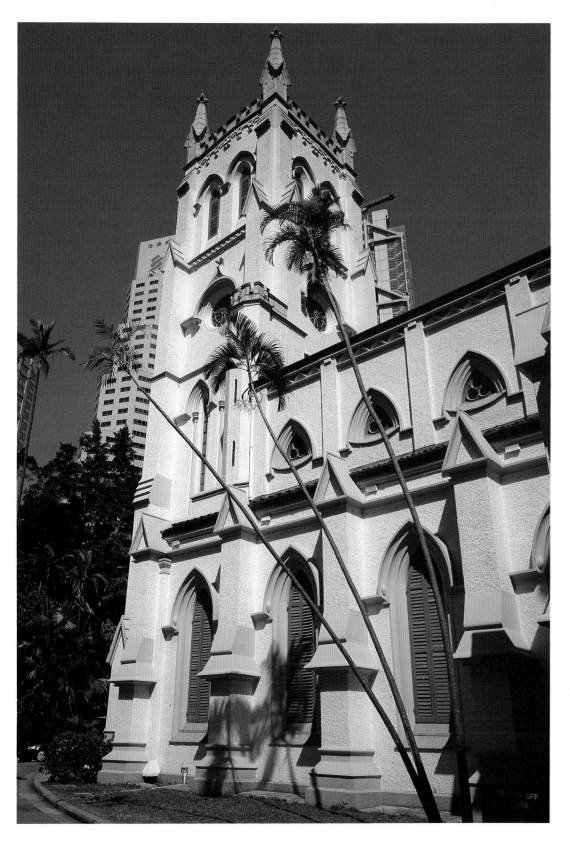

An Earlier Era, an Abiding Faith

*I*n 1997 St John's Cathedral, one of Hong Kong's oldest buildings and its only parcel of freehold land, will celebrate its 150th anniversary.

A short stroll from the glass canyons of Central, the Cathedral precinct is shaded by banyons and palms and is a retreat for cockatoos and parrots, the occasional t'ai chi practitioner and those who enjoy the atmosphere of calm that clings to this part-Gothic, part-Norman landmark.

Those who wander into its cool interior take pleasure from its air of repose, the glow of its stained-glass windows and the sheen of rosewood and teak pews. The Cathedral's first service was held in March of 1849, two years after the foundation stone was laid. Prior to its erection, services – the first on Christmas Eve of 1843 – had been conducted in a matshed church.

St John's distinctive tower once rose against a sheer backdrop of tropical greenery, but today the city surrounds it. Flanked to the fore by two of Hong Kong's most spectacular contemporary towers, the Bank of China and the Hongkong and Shanghai Bank, it depends on its nearest neighbour, the old French Mission building, to complement its historic atmosphere with shutters and colonial arches. The Cathedral has survived a good deal, including being turned into a social club by the Japanese during the occupation. Stripped of its stained-glass windows, polished alters and choir stalls, and with its tower torn apart by a shell hole, the Cathedral reflected the destruction and plunder that was widespread in Hong Kong. However, the ravages of war were repaired, the interior refurbished and today St John's is both a reminder of another era and an abiding faith. 🦁

A Retreat for the Elite

*L*ife at the top of Victoria's scenic Peak became an attractive and practical alternative with the opening in 1888 of the Peak Tram. Though a heavy landslide nearly sent the tramway's first operators into liquidation, the funicular railway that ran between Garden Road and Victoria Gap – 397 metres above sea level – soon became one of Hong Kong's most famous landmarks.

Since 1901, the Governor had maintained a spectacular summer lodge on the Peak's summit and the front seat of the tram was always reserved for him. On arrival at Victoria Gap, liveried sedan-chair bearers would carry him on the 15-minute journey to Mountain Lodge. In 1907 Lady Lugard, the Governor's wife, noted that "the air grew cooler every minute" as the sedans swayed along the narrow mountain road to the manicured lawns, tennis courts and the flower-filled gardens of her summer retreat.

The Peak Reservation Ordinance of 1904 restricted residence on the Peak to those approved by the Governor – so only the socially acceptable could live with a view of one of the world's most spectacular harbours stretched out before them. A view which today costs just the price of a ticket on the Peak Tram.

48

49

The Sheen of Silk and Sweating Flanks

On an island that seemed to survive on gambler's good luck, the creation of Hong Kong's first racecourse inevitably followed soon after the colony's foundation. In the green folds of mosquito-infested Happy Valley, a scenic swathe of land was drained and levelled and hefty sums were soon being wagered on the small China ponies that raced around the track. The annual Chinese New Year races became a gala social occasion attracting everyone from the Governor and taipans to compradors and coolies and amahs.

The taipans entertained lavishly in refreshment booths surrounding the track, and the view from the grandstand – of swaggering soldiers, ladies dressed to the height of fashion, Chinese silks, shiny top hats and prancing imported ponies – ensured that this rare opportunity for leisure, and hopefully profit, was relished by all. Wrote the *London Times* in 1858: "If anyone is desirous of seeing good steady, old-fashioned racing where every horse is ridden to win, I am afraid he must go to Hong Kong!" Racing commenced at Happy Valley in 1845, and the taipans spared no expense in importing and training horses for the contests. China ponies – with "fire in their hearts" – raced alongside ponies from the Philippines and Australia. The Hong Kong Derby was first raced in 1873 and was confined to China pony griffins. Although imported thoroughbreds would later enhance the status of racing in Hong Kong, for many years the track was dominated by the spirited China ponies.

The shimmer of satin and the sheen of sweating flanks continue to lure crowds to Happy Valley and Hong Kong's second racetrack at Sha Tin in the New Territories. The season reaped the Royal Hong Kong Jockey Club well over HK$50 billion last year – boosting Government revenue by over $4 billion and providing local charities, recreation, higher education and other worthy causes with an injection of over $880 million. Over three million punters flocked to the two tracks during the September to June season. However, in the heat of summer the frenzied pursuit of punting profits is briefly forgotten and the pampered imported horses retreat to air-conditioned stables at the territory's tracks. 🦁

Memories of Tragedy

"*T*he races afforded great pleasure – the Chinese are as much excited as the English and bet with much ardour", noted the *Illustrated London News*. But tragedy destroyed the carnival atmosphere of the annual races in 1918. Fanned by strong winds, fire swept through the temporary matshed stands erected each year for this major event, and 600 were trapped and perished in the inferno. On a green hillside in Sookunpoo Valley, a shrine for those buried together on this spot is remembered by relatives of those who died in the fire. Joss sticks and prayers are still offered on the anniversary of the tragedy.

IN MEMORY
OF THOSE WHO
PERISHED IN THE
RACE COURSE
FIRE ON
FEBRUARY 26TH
1918

The Reigning Monarch …

Hong Kong received its first royal visit – a relatively informal affair – when Prince Alfred, Duke of Edinburgh, called in to inspect the progress of the fledgling colony while on a world tour in 1869. Since then, Hong Kong has welcomed many a royal visitor, but the pomp and ceremony reached unprecedented heights when, in early 1975, the Queen became the first British sovereign to visit the territory. Eleven years later she became the first reigning monarch to visit China and, in Hong Kong, noted that her visit symbolized a new relationship between Britain and China, a relationship in which the agreement over Hong Kong has played a significant part. "You have been promised", she said, "that the institutions, traditions and way of life so important to the people of Hong Kong will be preserved. The agreement and the firm commitments of the governments of the United Kingdom and China enshrined in it will, I trust, be an assurance and encouragement to you as you face the challenges of the future".

The despondency and uncertainty that had enveloped Hong Kong through the latter months of 1989 seemed briefly banished by the dazzling smile of a princess and the easy charm and assurance of the heir to the British throne when the royal yacht *Brittania* docked at HMS Tamar in November of that year. And if some detected a certain irony in the Gurkha Band's spirited rendition of "There'll always be an England", they never allowed the thought to darken the day.

Despite a hectic official schedule, the three-day visit was marked by an informality which would have delighted an earlier royal visitor. The Prince of Wales pictured (*right*) taking the royal salute on his arrival in Hong Kong in 1922 and seen with Governor Stubbs and the Earl of Mountbatten (*following page*) shared with the current heir (*pictured on page 57*), on his arrival in Hong Kong in 1992 with Governor Patten a passion for polo and indicated to his hosts that lengthy official banquets were anathema to him. Lady Stubbs must have been greatly relieved as the colony was temporarily crippled by a seamen's strike at the time. 🦁

Of Egret Plumes and Trilbies…

Spectacle had always been an intrinsic element of Empire. In India, in the days of the Raj, it was peacock feather fans and elephants caparisoned in gold. On the colonial island of Hong Kong it was splendid sedan chairs carried by bearers in livery, and immaculate parades featuring the Governor of the day attired in white colonial dress and a solar topee topped with pure white egret plumes. The latter became as much a part of the colonial spectacle as the billowing Union Jack or the 17-gun salute that welcomed a new Governor, and its absence was liable to cause consternation, speculation or more recently jubilation. Most Governors chose to sport the plumed helmet and a break with tradition tended to heighten the theatrical effect of a prop worthy of a Gilbert and Sullivan comic opera. Some Governors clearly considered such protection from the midday sun an essential part of the colonial panoply, others shunned it and seldom donned or doffed it. Sir Andrew Caldecott opted for a top hat, photographed on his arrival as Governor of Hong Kong in 1935 *(right)*. Japan's wartime Governors predictably replaced it with battledress headgear. More recently, Sir Edward Youde abandoned it in favour of a military dress hat. Sir Robert Black *(inset)* chose to wear full summer uniform and solar topee in welcoming Princess Alexander at Kai Tak airport in 1963.

And when Hong Kong's 28th Governor arrived to assume his post as the colony's last Governor, there was a ceremonial welcome conducted with full pomp and pageantry – but not an egret feather in sight! When he crossed the harbour to an official welcome from knights of the realm, a baroness and other dignitaries with honours, Mr Chris Patten simply wore an elegant business suit. Local pundits predicated problems for cartoonists and photographers who had long relished portraying Hong Kong's Governor in a plumed helmet – particularly in a high wind. Those given to analysing the significance of symbols spoke of a break with the past, the dawn of a new era. When Mr Patten took the traditional oaths – vowing to serve the Queen and the people of Hong Kong – he later amplified his commitment to representing the interests of the people of Hong Kong. "I will stand up for Hong Kong as you would wish me to do, courteously and firmly", he said. But clearly not in a plumed helmet.

From Silver Candelabra to Shoji Screens

In Victorian Hong Kong the socially ambitious lived in the hope of receiving a gilt-edged invitation to one of the grand occasions that marked the social calendar at Government House. Garden parties, receptions and balls, all catered for with the finest fare the colony could provide, made Government House the centre of Hong Kong's social life. Those who loved to dance noted that its ballroom could amply accommodate at least 12 sets of dancers for the quadrille and, with lanterns strung across its darkening gardens, a ball at Government House became a picturesque affair, a lingering memory.

Government House was built in 1853 – prior to that, the first Governors had to find their own rented mansions on which the accolade "Government House" was briefly bestowed.

During the Second World War, the neoclassical colonial mansion acquired its current unique blend of European and Japanese architectural styles. Recognizing that the structure had been weakened by an air raid tunnel built beneath it by the British, and wishing his new home to reflect his own culture, the Japanese Governor embarked on an ambitious rebuilding programme. Being a master of the tea ceremony, the Governor's own suite reflected this passion and featured raised floors and shoji screens.

Such embellishments found little favour with Hong Kong's first peace-time Governor, Admiral Harcourt, whose fleet had sailed into the war-torn city on 30th August 1945, and who later read the Surrender Document to the heads of the occupying forces in the new tiered and turreted Government House. Shoji screen and Formosan pine were jettisoned, to be replaced by more traditional trappings – gleaming candelabra and crystal, the sheen of polished wood and silver, flowered cretonnes and portraits of the reigning monarch to whom Hong Kong had been restored as seen in the main dining room.

Slogans Beneath the Noonday Sun

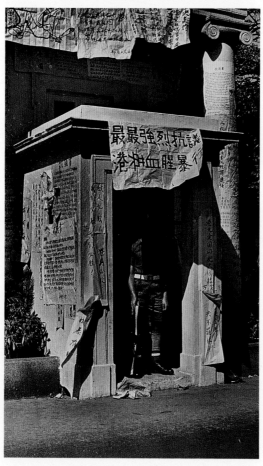

Usually the imposing entrance to Government House witnesses the arrival and departure of impressive limousines bearing VIPs and guests to and from the mansion that has become synonymous with British colonial rule.

However, during the summer of 1967 the entrance became the venue for a series of demonstrations that further raised tensions in a city already living through Communist riots.

Anti-colonial propaganda was plastered on the walls, Mao books were raised in unison and agitators in their familiar blue and white attire chanted the challenge of their slogans beneath the noonday sun and the unflinching gaze of British soldiers mounting guard at the firmly closed gates.

The Stepping Stone of History

The stone steps of Government House have, over the years, become a convenient place for photographs of visiting dignitaries such as the Viceroy of Canton, Chang Jen Chuh, who visited the colony early this century and was the guest of the then Governor, Sir Frederick Lugard.

The steps serve the same photographic purpose for the Governor, Lord Wilson, in office in the early 1990s as Hong Kong enters what must be the most crucial decade of its turbulent existence.

With worldwide attention focused on the future of the last major British colony, Lord and Lady Wilson are photographed flanked by their sons, the Governor's personal Aide-de-camp and Honorary Aides representing branches of the disciplined services stationed in Hong Kong.

The Land-hungry Colony

An early Armenian entrepreneur, Sir Paul Chater, first advocated reclaiming land in Central to accommodate both the Supreme Court and Royal Square.

Such was the scale of its development, on a daily basis, that even in its infancy Hong Kong sought to advance its harbour frontage to create the level land needed to accommodate a fast-growing city port. Given the sheer and unyielding nature of the emerald flanked mountain that rose above the Victorian city – and was soon studded with colonnaded colonial mansions – Hong Kong embarked upon an ambitious programme of reclamation which continues into the 20th century to radically change the contours of its shoreline and harbour.

Projects currently on the drawing board aim to add substantial land stocks to prime areas of Central and Kowloon, narrowing the span of the harbour, but increasing an asset that is increasingly in short supply.

Seventy years span the passage of time between these two views looking east down Des Voeux Road Central, named after Sir William Des Voeux, who served the Colony as governor from 1887 – 1891.

Star Ferry Terminal

Once Kowloon and the New Territories had been ceded to Hong Kong, cross harbour transportation multiplied, prompting the need for a ferry service. Prominent hotelier Dorabjee Nowrojee (*above*), who was already obligingly ferrying friends and customers back and forth across the harbour, decided to expand this unofficial service and in 1897 the first Star Ferry – *The Evening Star* – made its maiden harbour crossing. Despite the introduction of the Cross-Harbour Tunnel and the Mass Transit Railway, the Star Ferry's 12 vessels still do brisk business – offering commuters and tourists alike a view of one of the world's most scenic harbours while carrying them to their destinations which perhaps explains why the ferries are still the preferred mode of transport for well over 40 million passengers annually.

Sailing Through History

*B*utterfly-sailed junks, with weather-worn timbers and cluttered decks, chased shoals across the South China Seas for centuries, until technology rendered their picturesque sails redundant. The sea gypsies – who were veritable Noah's Arks of humans and animals – were Hong Kong's first inhabitants. Forming permanent fishing communities in the bays of Hong Kong Island, the boat people in their junks once shared the waters with notorious pirates until the British Navy began to police the coastal waters when Hong Kong was ceded to Britain. As in South China, vast floating populations created a colourful bustle around harbours such as Aberdeen and Yau Ma Tei where mighty junks with wide peaked sails moved among smaller riverine junks and squat sampans. Junks have sailed through China's long history, and their silhouettes on the horizon as they sail past the corporate headquarters of the China Trade are the last reminders of a less hurried era in Hong Kong's history.

The Orient Express

A solitary clock tower – all that remains of the Kowloon-Canton Railway Terminus – is a reminder of an early, unhurried era of travel. From the 1930s the railway was linked to the Trans-Siberian and those wishing to avoid the six-week steamer trip from Hong Kong to England could opt for plush, wood-panelled luxury – and plenty of samovar tea – crossing China and Russia to Paris. With only a few carriage changes, rail passengers could disembark at Victoria Station 18 days after leaving Hong Kong. When the Kowloon-Canton Terminus opened in 1910 it marked Hong Kong's first transportation link with the interior of China. Foreign consortiums, some based in Hong Kong, vied with one another for the rights to construct railways across China. However, the iron arteries that soon fed China's major cities and opened up new areas to trade and travel were often bitterly resented. Those long engaged in carrying both people and cargo across China on more basic forms of transport – from barges to carts and sedans – could not hope to compete with the smoke-belching trains that shrieked across once-undisturbed tracts of China's interior. As such, railways became, for some, bitter symbols of foreign incursions into China, and a focus for attack when anti-foreign resentment erupted. Even the Emperor had difficulty accepting the ear-piercing whistles that announced the passing of trains.

On sacred days, such as the winter solstice Sacrifice to Heaven, when he lead a pre-dawn procession from the Forbidden City to the Temple of Heaven, he ordered citizens along his route to stay indoors and shutter their windows – and banned all rail traffic. Thus no 20th-century sound could disturb an ancient ritual of communication between the Emperor of China and Heaven.

Though the Trans-Siberian Railway reduced travelling time to Europe, most colonials opted for the six-week sea voyage on shipping lines that had always linked early traders, taipans and colonial administrators with the distant island "home" they had left far behind. The Peninsular and Oriental Line began sailing into Singapore, Hong Kong and Shanghai from the mid-1840s. In the early days it was whispered that the P & O steamers, carrying high-minded Victorians in its mahogany and brass cabins, smuggled opium

in its hold – but such gossip merely added to the aura of a shipping line that became as much a part of Empire as curry tiffins at colonial clubs.

In fact, P & O steamers had a colonial club atmosphere, even coining a new word "posh". Seasoned colonial travellers, wishing to escape the worst of the tropic sun, selected their cabins "port out, starboard home" when travelling between England and Hong Kong.

In the 1920s, when the mail steamers arrived weekly, the wharf was always a social hub. Departing vessels were laden with flowers, festooned with streamers; while arrivals invariably brought to the wharf young men in straw boaters, eagerly scanning the decks for the face of a girlfriend, destined to be a bride within days – if she hadn't met another lucky fellow on the sea voyage out and disembarked at Singapore. 🦁

There was Once a Queen ...

When Cunard's luxury liner *Queen Elizabeth* sailed into Hong Kong harbour, the pride of Britain's transatlantic fleet invariably stirred great interest in the port.

As she moved majestically among rusting cargo ships, naval vessels, battered seagoing fishing junks and the hard-working tugs and sampans that crisscrossed the harbour – all acknowledged the arrival of a ship of awesome status. As was expected, she took her place in the waterfront's prime berth and enjoyed being the centre of so much admiring attention.

However, by the 1960s, with the world moving at a faster pace, air travel eclipsed the cruise ship's attractions and Cunard sold the huge liner to American entrepreneurs who turned her into a Florida tourist attraction doomed for failure.

Sold at auction, she was acquired by Hong Kong shipping magnate C.Y. Tung who nurtured a dream of giving the cruise ship a new lease of life as a floating university. But the millionaire's vision foundered when fire broke out on the vessel undergoing a HK$30 million refit in Hong Kong's harbour only weeks away from its maiden cruise.

Arson was suspected as several fires broke out simultaneously on 9th January 1972. Most of the 2,000 workmen had left for lunch, but 700 remained, including luncheon guests who had arrived to celebrate the venture about to be launched.

Fireboats converged on the liner; helicopters hovered overhead; and pleasure junks gathered to help evacuate the panic-stricken people who clustered on the main deck or leapt into the harbour waters. Within an hour most of the superstructure of the 83,000-ton liner was ablaze. Water from fireboats simply shrouded the vessel in billowing clouds of steam while the relentless fire raged on from stem to stern.

At night the great ship that had, in happier times, added glitter to the harbour, now glowed an angry red from every port

hole. Gas cylinders and light bulbs exploded and the flares from lifeboats, activated by the heat, lit the night sky with a macabre carnival brilliance.

For three days and nights she blazed. When there was nothing more to burn, a haunting stillness engulfed the harbour and the great gutted hulk turned on its side and churned the harbour waters for the last time. Firemen who had sprayed their fireboat hoses when the proud old liner had entered the harbour for its refit, stood to attention to mark the final moments of a great ship.

Those who watched the liner's demise knew it was not a fitting end for a grand lady of the seas that had known both luxury and hard times. For the *Queen Elizabeth* had used its 186,000 horsepower engines to outrun German submarines and evade torpedoes as a troop carrier before assuming her role as the world's fastest, most luxurious cruise ship, ferrying the *crème de la crème* to far-flung exotic ports.

The ship's steel and brass were eventually salvaged to live on in other structures and her spirit certainly survives – for the luxurious *QE II (previous pages)*, its passenger list studded with the world's richest, today regularly sails in and out of the harbour that claimed her famous predecessor.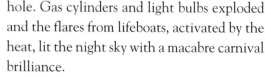

The Golden Mile's Yesterdays

Nathan Road, Kowloon's main thoroughfare, was once a breezy tree-lined boulevard, lined with colonial architecture, shaded by Banyans and bordered by Chinese flower gardens that flourished on the recumbent peninsula after it was ceded to Britain under the terms of the Treaty of Peking in 1862.

Named after Sir Mathew Nathan, the Colony's 13th Governor, who nurtured the optimistic vision of constructing a major highway that would reach Canton and ultimately stretch to Europe, but got no further than Boundary Street in Kowloon.

Today, the road is gaudy with neon and bustling with travellers in search of treasures of antiquity to space-age technologies. Nathan Road offers every imaginable temptation to indulge the acquisitive urge. Few can resist purchasing the latest in sophisticated electronic and photographic gadgetry in the tax-free shops that line the "Golden Mile" of Nathan Road.

"The Pen" and the Bay

In 1928, The Peninsula made its debut on the social scene and was quickly embraced as the favourite rendezvous for tycoons, travellers and gay young flappers in search of tea dances. At its opening an American lady observed: "I'd feel rich here if I hadn't a dime in my pocket!" – and everyone knew exactly what she meant.

However, one year prior to its opening, the hotel was being used to billet several thousand British troops brought from Singapore and India to face a possible Communist threat on the New Territories border. Strapping soldiers from a Guards Regiment drilling on Nathan Road, and receiving machine gun instruction on the hotel's verandah, did much to boost the spirits of locals – and just as much to damage the as yet undecorated hotel. Their presence in such a prominent and palatial "barracks" was apparently enough to avert further border troubles.

When the hotel opened its doors a year later it already seemed a familiar landmark and was dubbed "The Pen" by those who regularly attended its tea dances and balls.

"The Pen" had a distinctly ritzy atmosphere and in its famous gilt-ornamented lobby high society gathered to sip pink gins and stengahs and observe one another between pillars and palms, to the strains of a string quartet. It soon became unwritten law that married couples occupied the right side of the lobby whereas the unattached positioned themselves, in hopeful anticipation, on the left! The head waiter was on the alert to direct the uninitiated to the side of the lobby he felt most appropriate to their appearance.

By the time "The Pen" had established itself as the most fashionable venue for major social events, its sister hotel, the Repulse Bay, had already been discovered by the romantic. With its mountain backdrop and the scenic sweep of its blue bay (*following pages*), the hotel's spacious suites and deep-shaded verandah became a favourite summer place. Bathing huts lined the pale crescent of the beach, and after peerless sunsets the bay filled with the lanterns of hundreds of local fishing craft.

During the war both hotels played significant roles. House-to-house fighting in the mansions that studded Repulse Bay meant that many took refuge in the hotel until enemy troops began to close in on the immaculate tropical gardens. When the colony finally surrendered, a brief ceremony was held at The Peninsula after which the Governor was imprisoned in room 336. The hotel was renamed the Toa Hotel and was extensively used by the Japanese for entertaining.

First Impressions

*F*ly into Hong Kong's Kai Tak airport and your first impressions will be dramatically etched in the mind. Multi-storey apartment blocks festooned with laundry suddenly fill the aircraft window as your flight – one of over 600 that land each day – sails over the city, glides to rest on a runway jutting into the blue of Kowloon Bay, and offers you a panoramic view of one of the world's most dynamic cities. Kai Tak, one of the busiest international airports, owes its existence to a group of Chinese businessmen chasing real estate profits. Sir Ho Kai and Au Tak conceived the idea of filling in Kowloon Bay and building some 200 houses on the reclaimed Kai Tak Bund. However, rumours that the area was fever-infested inhibited interest and sent the company bankrupt, whereupon the land was resumed.

In the 1920s, a civilian airport was constructed and soon light aircraft were touching down – occasionally upside down. Pioneer aviators, viewing the colony's granite crests and craggy coastline, advocated the use of flying boats that required only a pier and landing stage tower. Certainly by the 1930s flying boats were a familiar sight, lying at anchor in the harbour. Flying boat passengers to London enjoyed the stengahs and sunsets from the verandahs of colonial hostelries in Siam, Burma, India the Persian Gulf and the Mediterranean.

When the first commercial flights landed at Kai Tak in the 1930s they literally stopped traffic for the runway cut across the main Kowloon road to the Sai Kung peninsula. Though initially accessible only to the wealthy traveller, a flight to London cost £360, twice as much as the steamer.

Known to be one of the safest airports in the world because of exacting landing procedures demanded of pilots, Kai Tak was, however, the scene of a freak mishap in 1990 when a Chinese-owned airliner overshot the runway (*above*) and broke up in the harbour with the loss of little life.

Kai Tak is today the world's sixth busiest airport and boasts the biggest air cargo facility. But the proximity of nearby residential buildings – that contribute to that unforgettable first impression – necessitate the closure of the airport to a midnight curfew. Its single runway, which can only be repaired during night hours, restricts the number of aircraft movements. An ambitious new two-runway airport, planned for sparsely populated Lantau Island, will eventually release Kai Tak land for the sort of property development originally envisaged for the site, by Ho Kai and Au Tak.

A Port in Need

It was Hong Kong's "safe and commodious harbour" that first lured the eye of Britain's Lord Napier, searching for an offshore base for the China Trade merchants. Soon the harbour, sheltered in the embrace of green hills, was accommodating trading ships from many nations, plus the gunboats that had helped win Britain an Empire that covered a quarter of the world.

At the height of Empire, British vessels were never far from a British port with docks, coaling stations and naval bases. The growth of the China Trade ensured that industries linked with trade – ship building and repairing – also flourished.

By the turn of the century the colony could build ships faster than any competitor and was challenging Britain's supremacy in this field. Today, however, with harbour-front land ranked as some of the world's most expensive real estate, ship building is no longer a major industry and most dry dock facilities have all but disappeared.

"A Safe and Commodious Harbour..."

Despite a peerless, sheltered harbour pronounced "safe and commodious" by Britain's Lord Napier when the colony was established, Hong Kong was subjected to seasonal typhoons that tore up bricks and mortar and matshed, scattered and sank trading and fishing vessels, and claimed the lives of thousands. In infancy, the colony was subjected to the first of the Big Winds which totally destroyed the townsite and then rounded back on itself to tear up much of the repair work.

Often there was little warning of the typhoons that swept up from the Philippines – though later on Jesuit fathers manning the Manila weather bureau would be able to warn Hong Kong's Observatory of their approach. In 1874, small craft were peacefully plying the harbour's waters in the afternoon, but by midnight one of the colony's worst typhoons was ripping off rooftops, uprooting trees, smashing fishing craft against the praya wall and casting steamers onto the waterfront. The screams of those whose houses or boats were being destroyed rose above the sounds of the raging storm and 2,000 lives were lost in the space of six hours.

From Penance to Proud Tradition

British songwriter Sir Noël Coward (*right*), whose career in musical theatre carried him throughout Asia, celebrated Hong Kong's noonday gun in a song about the extraordinary eccentricities of "Mad Dogs and Englishmen". Britain was about to shed her empire – but Hong Kong being the exception to the rule, the noonday gun survived along with the colony. Today, it is still fired by Jardine's – a tradition begun in the early years when a merchant prince was accorded a royal salute by his staff on arrival in the harbour – much to the disgust of colonial officials.

Hong Kong's most powerful hong agreed to fire a cannon at noon each day – and what was once a penance has now become a proud tradition, and something of a talisman!

From its earliest days, Hong Kong's defence depended on the strategically placed guns that guarded both harbour and border.

However, when the time came for the colony to defend itself against battle-hardened Japanese forces, the territory once dubbed "a fortress" proved to be lamentably ill-equipped. As Japanese tanks, artillery, infantry and cavalry crossed the New Territories' border, defence forces – backed by civilian volunteers – retreated to the island for what the BBC described as "an old-fashioned siege".

The colony finally surrendered on Christmas Day, 1941, and was occupied until 30th August 1945, when the Hong Kong Government received its first communique since the Union Jack had been lowered:

"Rear Admiral Harcourt is lying outside Hong Kong with a very strong fleet..."

Today, field guns that once saw action in defence of the territory are now curiosities outside the New Territories' Police Headquarters. 🦁

Gateway to the Past

Not surprisingly the "Sport of Kings" held great attractions for Hong Kong's merchant princes and, when Jardine and Matheson's Number One House rose on a tree-shaded hillside overlooking the harbour, at East Point, the taipan's stables were not far away. Just as Number One House boasted the colony's finest imported chefs and wines, so its stables accommodated some of its fastest and most spirited imported ponies.

The rivalry between the hongs that dominated Hong Kong invariably spilled over to the racetrack where family, friends and staff indicated their support for a particular stable of ponies by reflecting its racing colours in the attire they chose for the annual races.

Number One House stood on a site purchased at the colony's first land auction in 1841. In 1923, it was purchased from Jardine's by a leading Chinese businessman, Lee Hysan, and was the scene of the wedding of his daughter in the mid-1930s. The site would later accommodate the Lee Gardens Hotel to be replaced by an office block.

However, the great stone archway that marked the entrance to the company's stables was rebuilt, stone by stone, at Beas River Country Club, as a link with Hong Kong's racing past. The Country Club's stables currently accommodate over 150 retired racehorses – some used for recreation, some trained for dressage and showjumping. Their stables – once army barracks – are destined to become one of Asia's foremost equestrian centres.

Sisters of the Poor

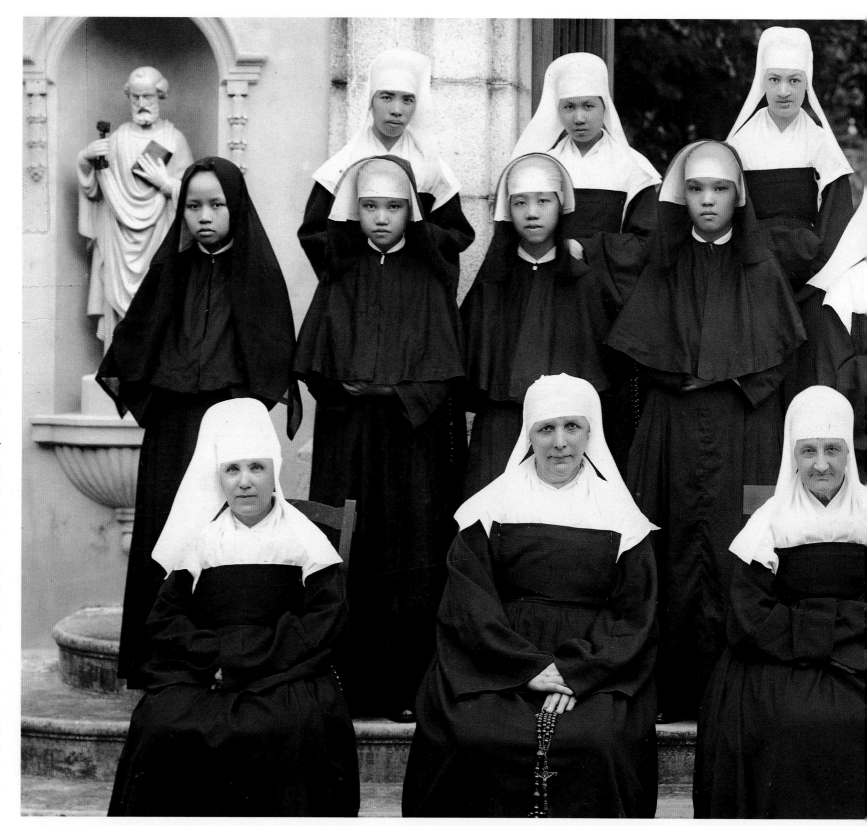

In May of 1848 four Catholic Sisters – three of them French, one English – left the familiar walls of their convent in Chartres and embarked on a sea voyage half way across the world to a tiny fever-infested island that had soon claimed the life of at least one of them. Four months later, sailing into Hong Kong harbour, locals noted their strange black-and-white habit, their calm faces and the starched white coifs that so resembled lotus flowers.

Talk of the Sisters of St Paul of Chartres mounted when they established themselves not in the comfortable punkah-cooled colonial accommodation favoured by foreigners, but on a humid hillside shack in Wan Chai.

The Sisters were among the first to establish their Catholic order in the new town site of Hong Kong and word soon spread that they would take in the children routinely abandoned on the streets – because they were girls, because they were sick or because of poverty.

"In those days the Sisters – trying to conform to Chinese custom – did not dare to venture out much because their habit was so distinctive", says Sister Pauline, Provincial Superior of St Paul's Convent today. "So at first they sent a priest into the streets to collect the abandoned children and bring them to the orphanage".

Soon, however, people brought their children to the Asile de la Sainte Enfance, often starving or ill, sometimes just in time to have them baptised by the Bishop and buried at the order's expense. Eventually the Sisters abandoned the sedan chairs in which they ventured out, and took to walking through the fast-growing town. When the order outgrew its early accommodation, it acquired an old cotton mill between the racecourse and the polo ground at Causeway Bay – and this was transformed into a complex comprising an orphanage, a convent and an Anglo-French school in 1914. It was to this complex, dominated by the granite dome of St Paul's Cathedral, that Sister Helena, now 84, arrived in 1934.

"Being local Portuguese I could speak English and a smattering of French, so I often acted as a translator. Eventually I became a novice – I had always wanted to join an order because my family has been connected with the Catholic church for generations and my father used to teach English to the French, Spanish and Italian missionaries. Later I myself would teach the novices, and today many of my students are heads of departments here. They still call me Mother!" laughs Sister Helena.

During the war years she remembers taking refuge in the basement, and of hastily transforming the chapel into a casualty ward for the mounting wounded.

Today, Sister Helena's hands are crippled by arthritis and she has spent the last few years confined to a wheelchair. But she makes light of her ailments, her hands occasionally reaching for the ivory rosary that is always twisted around the arms of her chair.

"I feel very much a part of the family of St Paul's", she observes simply, "and that is my chief pleasure in life now".

Pictured (*opposite page*) is Sister Helena with Sister Josephine back in the 1930s with a group of orphans at St Paul's. The photograph was found in London's Imperial War Museum. At the time of its discovery, there were no clues to its identity or location. Finally, after a long search it was shown to Sister Pauline who was delighted to announce that the two nuns featured in the photograph were still alive and well. The revelation called for a matching picture featuring both nuns on the same tiled verandah.

Outside the distant shrill of children's voices rise around the dome of St Paul's – as they always have. The orphans are long gone, and today the voices come from thousands of school children, in neat red and white uniforms, attending the order's school.

Sister Helena maneuvers her chair with hands as gnarled as some of the old banyans that shade the cathedral precinct. She has been discussing the political situation in South Africa, the extraordinary capacity of modern computers with some visitors to St Paul – but now it is eight o'clock and time to go to mass.

Aesop's Fables and Chinese Classics

Queen's College, one of Hong Kong's best-known schools, has had three names and four different locations, but the ideals that were at work when The Central School opened its doors in the 1860s still live on in the contemporary King's Road College. The school accepted its first contingent of pupils amidst the atmosphere of racial distrust that was a legacy of the Anglo-Chinese Wars. Its founders, Dr James Legge and Dr Frederick Stewart, both scholars with a profound respect for Chinese culture, were determined that their school would bridge the racial gap. Soon Chinese students sporting queues, some of them married men with families, were translating Aesop's Fables while British, Indian, Portuguese students were reciting the Chinese classics.

However, the school was subjected to the constant noisy clamour of the growing city and in 1876 a new site in Aberdeen Street was selected.

In April of 1884, a student destined to play a leading role in shaping the turbulent future of China, Sun Yat-sen, enrolled at The Central School.

No doubt he was impressed with the imposing granite building that emerged – large, lofty classrooms, and "a spacious noble hall capable of seating 1,000". The Great Hall, with its Ionic pilasters and honour

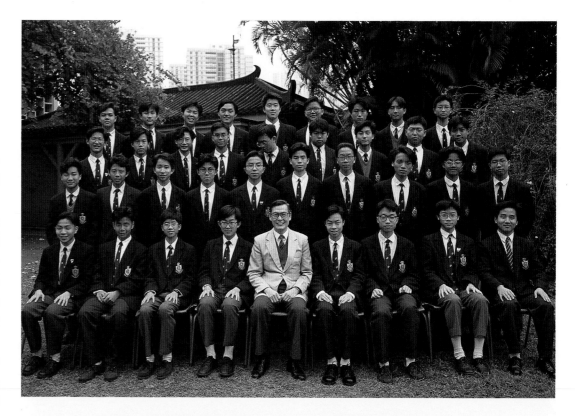

boards bearing the names of generations of scholars, was used for lectures, feasts and major examinations.

This once famous landmark, so much a part of the collective memory of local students, did not, however, survive the war-time occupation of the colony. After the fall of Hong Kong it became the headquarters of a contingent of Japanese cavalry who turned desks into feed boxes.

When they abandoned the building, once dubbed "The Old Lady of Aberdeen Street", looters converged ripping out floorboards and posts for firewood. A fire completed its undignified destruction, and when former pupils sought out their old school they found only rubble.

As postwar Hong Kong picked itself up, so did the school. Temporary accommodation was found and in 1950 the Governor, Sir Alexander Grantham, laid the foundation stone for the present College in King's Road, Causeway Bay, opposite Victoria Park. 🦁

Father's Pride

*I*n China, the lattice work of family ties has always spelt security and continuity – be it in the tending of rice fields by clans whose survival has always been tied to the land, or in the running of business empires that have spanned generations and accumulated extraordinary wealth and prestige. Skills and wealth passed down from father to son, through generations of Chinese families, as naturally as season followed season. Only now, in Hong Kong, are time-honoured family traditions being questioned by a generation exposed to the choices and challenges of higher education.

However, in the Fung Ping Fan family, the business empire established when Sir Kenneth's father came to Hong Kong, at the turn of the century, lives on in his son and grandson. The company – like the colony with which it has long been associated – has lived through fluctuating fortunes, and has survived. Today, the man at the helm of one of Hong Kong's renowned trading groups is much honoured, not only for his achievements in business, but for his social commitment. He is a Commander of the Most Excellent Order of the British Empire, and has twice been a recipient of the Order of the Sacred Treasure of Japan.

Parsees – Past and Present

Though British traders and Chinese merchants and compradors dominated the early years of the fledgling colony, Indian merchants were also quick to see the potential of the entrepôt port. The Parsees, in particular, established wholesale businesses and formed a community of considerable influence. One of the most famous early arrivals was Dorabjee Nowrojee, who began working as a cook and ended up a prosperous hotelier. He also founded the colony's most famous form of transport – the Star Ferry.

The Parsees were followed by Hindu and Muslim traders. Arriving from India in the 1890s, the Ruttonjee family were destined to play an important role in the commercial and social life of the city. The Ruttonjee Sanitorium and the Ruttonjee Centre are proud reminders of the family's vision and commitment. The Parsee community continues to prosper and contribute, with Keki Jokhi, Noshir Pavri and Jal Shroff *(right)* deriving obvious enjoyment from paralleling the past.

An Affinity with Beauty

Growing up in Peking, a city famous for the antique and curio shops that crowded its narrow streets, Charlotte Horstmann acquired an intuitive affinity for the treasures of China. She acknowledges that exploring such shops was part of the city's social life, so that, almost by osmosis, she learnt to detect the qualities inherent in the finest porcelains, bronzes and jade.

The distinguished scholar and collector and Charlotte's mentor, Otto Burckhart, encouraged her, and with him she was exposed to ancient treasures that had hardly seen daylight, so jealously had they been guarded.

In such a refined area, there is only so much you can acquire by learning – the rest comes through handling countless objects of infinite antiquity and by developing an instinctive response to such pieces.

The knowledge of Mandarin she acquired from her Chinese father, and her own acknowledged beauty, bestowed by a German mother, were obvious assets in a society that valued beauty above all else.

"She lived in a fine house on Sweet Water Well Lane", wrote a colleague observing her entrance at a Peking fancy dress party one evening soon after the revolution. "She came as a Manchu princess in an embroidered gown topped with a kingfisher feather tiara. We expected no less".

She left Peking in 1951, opened an antique shop in Bangkok and then came to Hong Kong – where the name Horstmann is still synonymous with the finest of Chinese antiques.

From Qing to Chanel

The beauty of the Orient is today born of a blend of old and new. In the past, Chinese women of status, encased in stiff embroidered silks, submitted mutely to the crippling practice of foot binding. Kept like birds in ornamental cages, they seldom saw the city that lay beyond the high, porcelain-tiled walls that enclosed their world. Occasionally they might venture into the city, but its colour and movement were only briefly glimpsed from behind the curtains of their fast-moving sedan chairs. Today, the status of women in Old China seems incredible to Hong Kong beauties, juggling challenges and choices, as they stride through city streets dressed in much the same way as their counterparts in Paris or New York.

But occasionally they opt for the infinite allure of embroidered silks and enveloping traditional gowns that allow them, for just a moment, a backward glance.

114

Golden Lily Feet

Chinese women of status were once proud of their "golden lily feet" – forcibly compressed since childhood to the three to five inches so enticing to men. Foot binding was initially designed to discourage women from straying – but later assumed an erotic appeal that won the practice and the compliance of those it crippled.

Only peasant women whose families could not afford to immobilize them and proud Manchu women, who had herded flocks on horseback in the harsh northern landscape, escaped a practice that became a symbol of social status. It is said that more than a few Manchu ladies would willingly have endured the pain to achieve the mincing "lily walk" of Chinese ladies – had not intermittent imperial edicts outlawed foot binding for China's rulers.

In the 1850s, the high-minded fanatics of the Taiping Rebellion banned foot binding along with queues, opium and prostitution, and later reformers also targeted the crippling practice. However, it was not officially banned until 1949 – when Chinese women had already taken their first steps on the road to emancipation.

Today, the tiny embroidered slippers that encased the seductive "golden lily feet" are mere curiosities of a long-gone era, occasionally arousing interest in the display cases of antique shops.

Accessories to Beauty

Chinese women have always taken pride in their glossy black hair that fell free, swung as a pigtail, was rolled into a bun or enticingly coiled and ornamented. Its elaborate designs could be held with stiffening resin; its sheen could be enhanced with dandelion oil. And, when lanterns lit the evening, old women, fanning themselves with palm leaves, would watch young girls coil and dress their hair, selecting first one, then another accessory – an antique jade or pearl pin, a precious pair of ornamental butterflies, a vivid kingfisher feather or a fresh flower. And a host of elegant accessories still turn the dressing of hair into an elaborate ritual.

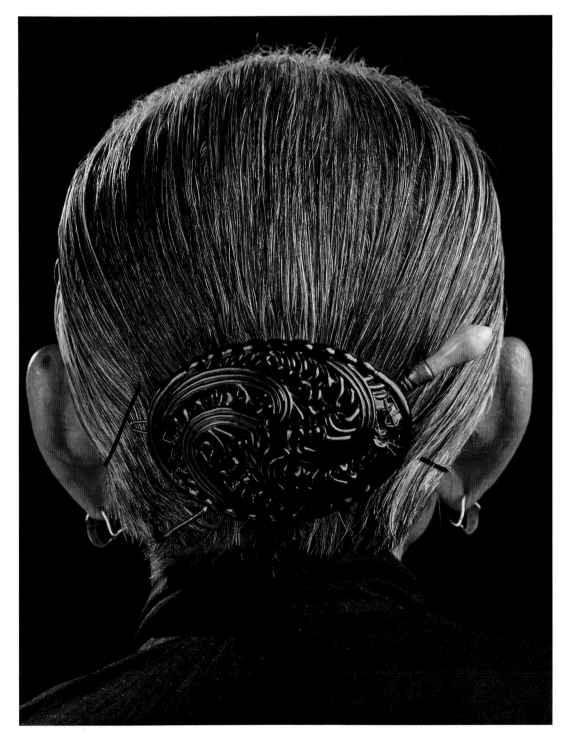

Chasing the Dragon

When Britain initially made trading overtures to China – having acquired a taste for China teas, silks and porcelain – the Emperor of the Middle Kingdom contemptuously dismissed invitations to purchase the proud new products of British industry. British traders, searching for a product to entice the China market and balance the China trade, found one in the vivid red acres of Bengal's poppy fields.

Opium had been mixed and smoked in China from the 17th century though its cultivation and import were banned by imperial decree. However, smuggled opium – "foreign mud" – succeeded in stemming the flow of silver bullion into China's coffers; was the catalyst for the conflict that won Britain Hong Kong; and hastened the fall of China's last dynasty by corrupting its officials and reducing even the Emperor's own eunuchs and bodyguards to hopeless addiction.

Opium fortunes financed the early vigorous growth of Hong Kong – but while the precocious imperial island was able to shake its financial dependence, the debilitating drug would prove fatal to many before being finally outlawed by both public opinion and official action.

In Hong Kong, some smoked opium at leisure in well-appointed divans where small white balls of hardened poppy sap were heated to release the sweet-scented coils of smoke that conjured such enticing dreams.

Others, seeking to ease weary limbs or escape poverty or despair, succumbed to "chasing the dragon" in dingy back alleys or smoke-veiled divans that would eventually claim their wasted bodies. Though opium addiction remains a legacy that continues to haunt Hong Kong, for most the pipes and paraphernalia of opium smoking have merely become the trappings of history.

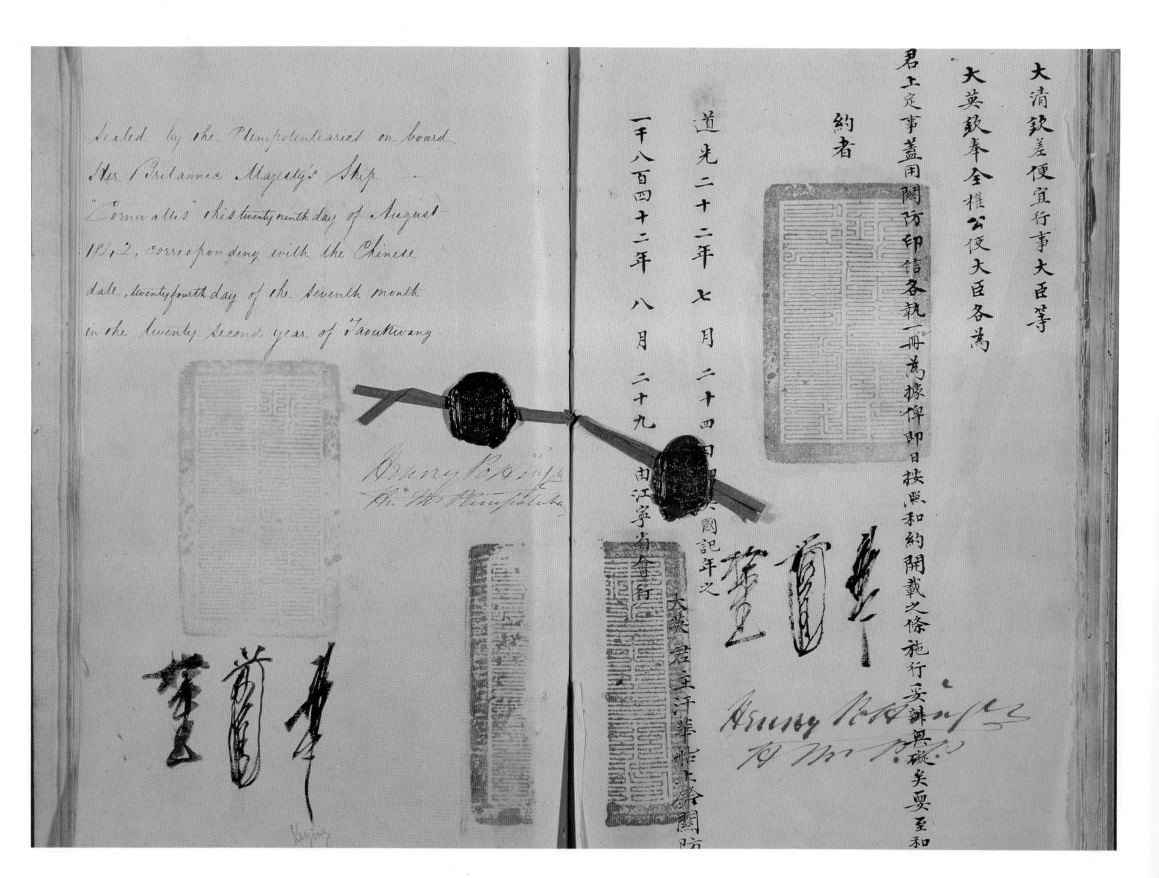

Sealed by the Plenipotentiaries on board
Her Britannic Majesty's Ship —
"Cornwallis" this twenty-ninth day of August
1842, corresponding with the Chinese
date, twentyfourth day of the seventh month
in the twenty second year of Taoukwang.

大清欽差便宜行事大臣等

大英欽奉全權公使大臣各為

君上定事蓋用關防印信各執一冊萬據悍即日按照和約開載之條施行妥辦無礙矣要至和

約者

道光二十二年七月二十四日即

英國記年之

一千八百四十二年八月二十九

由江寧省會行

大英君主汗華帖上蓋關防

The Brush Strokes of History

*I*t would seem to observers that Hong Kong has never been in a position to control its own destiny. A series of impressive official documents – replete with signatures, brush strokes, seals and chops – appeared to chart the course of its future when produced at landmark moments in its life.

Initially a pawn in a 19th-century conflict between two remote empires, Hong Kong was ceded in perpetuity to "Her Britannic Majesty, her heirs and successors" as part of the Treaty of Nanking. Mandarins in summer robes and uniformed British officials, in scarlet and blue, signed the Treaty *(left)* on the British flagship *HMS Cornwallis* moored in the Yangtze at Nanking on 29th August 1842.

To Britain, the island that promised a base of trade on the doorstep of China, was a symbol of the vision and enterprise of Empire. To China, its surrender festered as a source of bitter humiliation – the first stage in the dismantling of the once powerful Middle Kingdom.

When Japan, having observed the imperial powers at work in China, later began its own aggressive incursions into its neighbour in the 1930s, the last Manchu dynasty had already fallen and China was a republic. Japanese troops that had swept victoriously through China and Southeast Asia would eventually take the New Territories and Kowloon within four days, but Winston Churchill, urging Hong Kong's ill-equipped forces to fight on, intoned: "You guard a link long famous in world civilization between the Far East and Europe".

For a week before Christmas, 1941, the Japanese turned Hong Kong Island into a place of fire and smoke and thunder. Buildings were reduced to rubble, the harbour was littered with shattered vessels and narrow streets were choked with corpses.

On Christmas Day the colony finally surrendered; Government and civilian expatriates were herded into internment camps; and, as food shortages and privations mounted, thousands of Chinese fled back to their homeland. However, the dark shroud of occupation was lifted on 16th September 1945, when Vice Admiral Ruitaro Fujita and Major Umekichi Okada – seated at a small table bearing brushes and ink slab – signed the Surrender Document: "On behalf of the Emperor of Japan and the Japanese Imperial Headquarters, we do hereby unconditionally surrender ourselves and all forces under our control ...." The Japanese handed over their

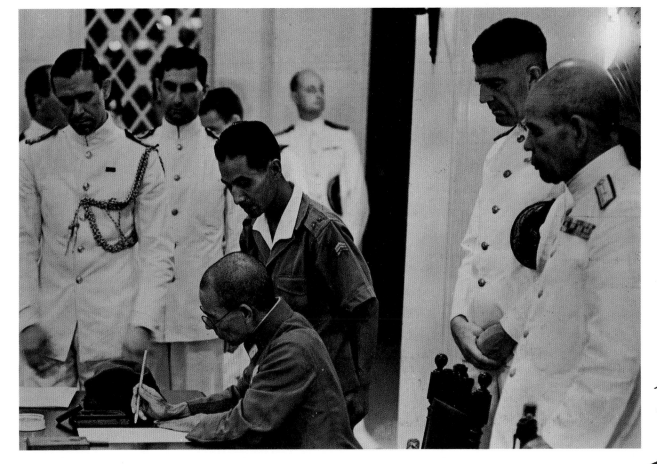

swords, bowed stiffly and were marched away from Government House.

The Royal Marine Band struck up the national anthem, an able seaman slowly hoisted the Union Jack, and in the harbour below warships thundered a salute, while the Fleet Air Arm roared approval overhead. Though the city lay in ruins, optimism ran as high as the energy that would rebuild the shattered colony.

陸軍少將

岡田梅吉

岡田

On behalf of the Government of the United Kingdom.

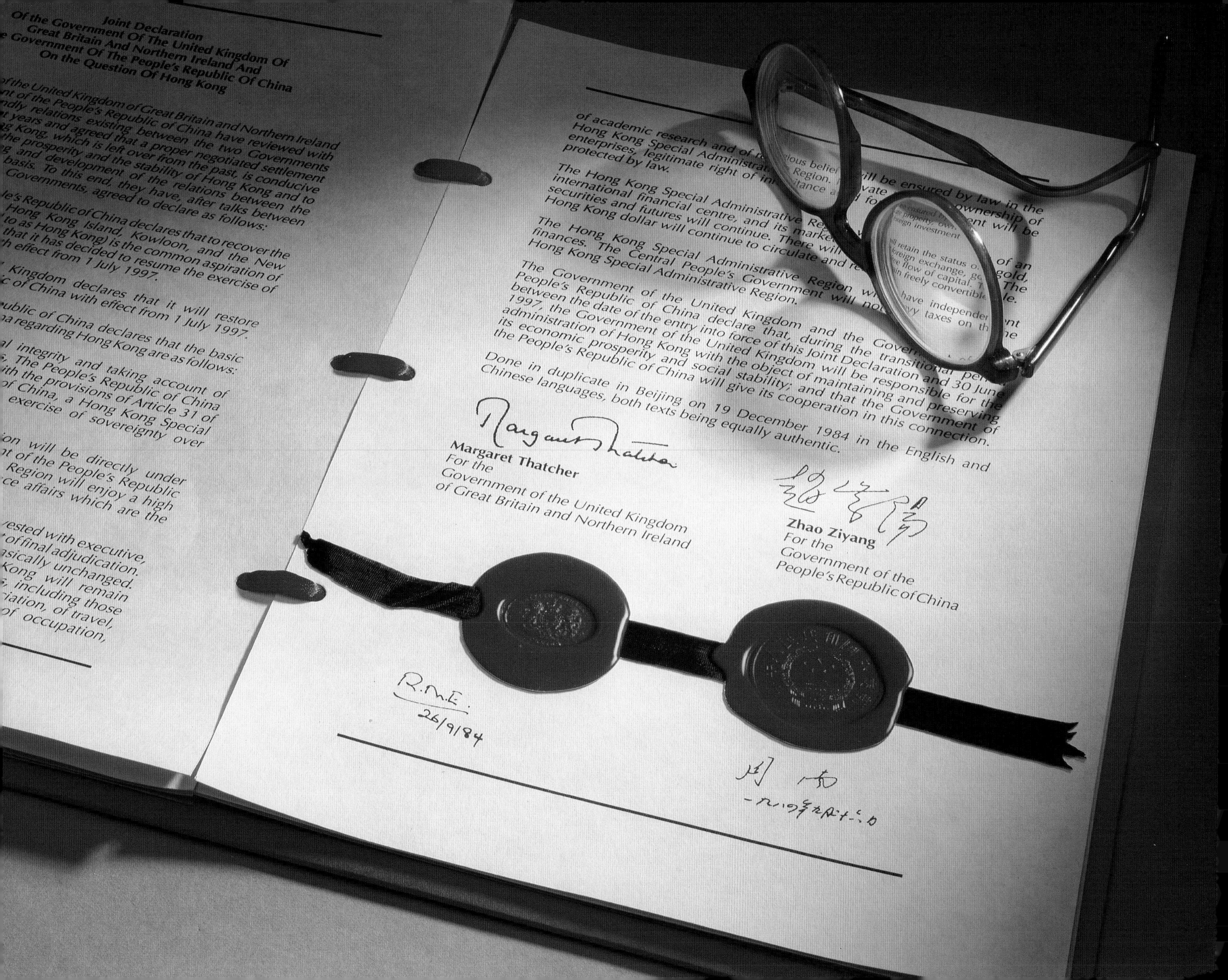

Joint Declaration
Of the Government Of The United Kingdom Of
Great Britain And Northern Ireland And
the Government Of The People's Republic Of China
On the Question Of Hong Kong

of the United Kingdom of Great Britain and Northern Ireland
nt of the People's Republic of China have reviewed with
ndly relations existing between the two Governments
t years and agreed that a proper negotiated settlement
g Kong, which is left over from the past, is conducive
the prosperity and the stability of Hong Kong and to
g and development of the relations between the
basis. To this end, they have, after talks between
Governments, agreed to declare as follows:

e's Republic of China declares that to recover the
Hong Kong Island, Kowloon, and the New
to as Hong Kong) is the common aspiration of
that it has decided to resume the exercise of
h effect from 1 July 1997.

Kingdom declares that it will restore
ic of China with effect from 1 July 1997.

blic of China declares that the basic
a regarding Hong Kong are as follows:

al integrity and taking account of
. The People's Republic of China
with the provisions of Article 31 of
of China, a Hong Kong Special
exercise of sovereignty over

ion will be directly under
t of the People's Republic
Region will enjoy a high
ce affairs which are the

ested with executive,
of final adjudication.
asically unchanged.
Kong will remain
, including those
iation, of travel,
f occupation,

of academic research and of r   ous belief   will be ensured by law in the
Hong Kong Special Administrati   e Region.   Private   ownership of
enterprises, legitimate right of in   itance a   d fo   foreign investment
protected by law.

The Hong Kong Special Administrative Reg
international financial centre, and its mark
securities and futures will continue. There w   ll retain the status o   of an
Hong Kong dollar will continue to circulate and re   foreign exchange, go   gold,
                                                         ree flow of capital.
The Hong Kong Special Administrative Region wi   n freely convertible   le.
finances. The Central People's Government will no   y taxes on th   e
Hong Kong Special Administrative Region.

The Government of the United Kingdom and the Govern
People's Republic of China declare that, during the transitional per
between the date of the entry into force of this Joint Declaration and 30 June
1997, the Government of the United Kingdom will be responsible for the
administration of Hong Kong with the object of maintaining and preserving
its economic prosperity and social stability; and that the Government of
the People's Republic of China will give its cooperation in this connection.

Done in duplicate in Beijing on 19 December 1984 in the English and
Chinese languages, both texts being equally authentic.

Margaret Thatcher
For the
Government of the United Kingdom
of Great Britain and Northern Ireland

Zhao Ziyang
For the
Government of the
People's Republic of China

R.M.E.
26/9/84

Almost 40 years later a third landmark document was signed in Beijing's Great Hall of the People by the Prime Minister of the People's Republic of China, Zhao Ziyang, and Britain's Prime Minister, Margaret Thatcher.

The date on this document was 19th December 1984 – and the mood it unleashed in Hong Kong was bleak. Nineteen ninety-seven – the date that the fast-living, hard-working colonial island had always pushed to the back of its collective psyche – had become a reality. The bottom fell out of the real estate market; the stock market plummeted; and long queues began to form outside foreign embassies. Though the Joint Declaration (*left*) promises the continued security of its freewheeling capitalist system for half a century, Hong Kong has long suspected that carefully worded documents – signatures, brush strokes, chops and seals – while appearing to determine a destiny, are merely part of a myriad of forces that have always been at work forging its future.